Baby Animals in the Wild!

Hippopotamus Calves in the Wild

by Marie Brandle

Bullfrog Books

Ideas for Parents and Teachers

Bullfrog Books let children practice reading informational text at the earliest reading levels. Repetition, familiar words, and photo labels support early readers.

Before Reading

- Discuss the cover photo. What does it tell them?

- Look at the picture glossary together. Read and discuss the words.

Read the Book

- "Walk" through the book and look at the photos. Let the child ask questions. Point out the photo labels.

- Read the book to the child, or have him or her read independently.

After Reading

- Prompt the child to think more. Ask: Hippopotamuses have body parts that help them live in the water. What are they?

Bullfrog Books are published by Jump!
5357 Penn Avenue South
Minneapolis, MN 55419
www.jumplibrary.com

Library of Congress Cataloging-in-Publication Data

Names: Brandle, Marie, 1989– author.
Title: Hippopotamus calves in the wild / by Marie Brandle.
Description: Minneapolis, MN: Jump!, Inc., [2023]
Series: Baby animals in the wild!
Includes index. | Audience: Ages 5–8
Identifiers: LCCN 2022010060 (print)
LCCN 2022010061 (ebook)
ISBN 9798885240710 (hardcover)
ISBN 9798885240727 (paperback)
ISBN 9798885240734 (ebook)
Subjects: LCSH: Hippopotamus—Infancy—Juvenile literature.
Classification: LCC QL737.U57 B725 2023 (print)
LCC QL737.U57 (ebook)
DDC 599.63/5—dc23/eng/20220317
LC record available at https://lccn.loc.gov/2022010060
LC ebook record available at https://lccn.loc.gov/2022010061

Editor: Eliza Leahy
Designer: Molly Ballanger

Photo Credits: Netta Arobas/Shutterstock, cover; Eric Isselee/Shutterstock, 1, 3, 12, 22 (bottom), 23bl, 24; Stu Porter/Shutterstock, 4, 23tr; Stephan Raats/Shutterstock, 5; Maciej Czekajewski/Shutterstock, 6–7; Gallo Images/Alamy, 8–9; Goddard_Photography/iStock, 10–11; ZSSD/Minden Pictures/SuperStock, 13, 23br; Animals Animals/SuperStock, 14–15; LouisLotterPhotography/Shutterstock, 16–17; Ed Short/Shutterstock, 18; YolandaVanNiekerk/iStock, 19, 23tl; Ann and Steve Toon/Alamy, 20–21; Shazzashaw/iStock, 22 (top).

Printed in the United States of America at Corporate Graphics in North Mankato, Minnesota.

Table of Contents

Life in the Water

This is a baby hippopotamus.
We call it a calf.

It stays with Mom.

Hippos live in Africa.

It is hot.

Africa

Water keeps hippos cool.
They stand in it most
of the day.

The calf has gray skin.
Mom cleans it.

The calf has a long muzzle.

muzzle ·····▶

Nostrils are on top.

They close underwater!

nostril

13

Eyes are high on hippos' heads.

Why?

This lets them see above the water!

Hippos leave the water to eat.

They eat grass.

Then they rest!
Mud keeps them cool.

mud

The calf and Mom join the group.

It is called a bloat.

bloat

The calf grows.

It will be as heavy as a car someday!

Parts of a Hippopotamus Calf

What are the parts of a hippopotamus calf? Take a look!

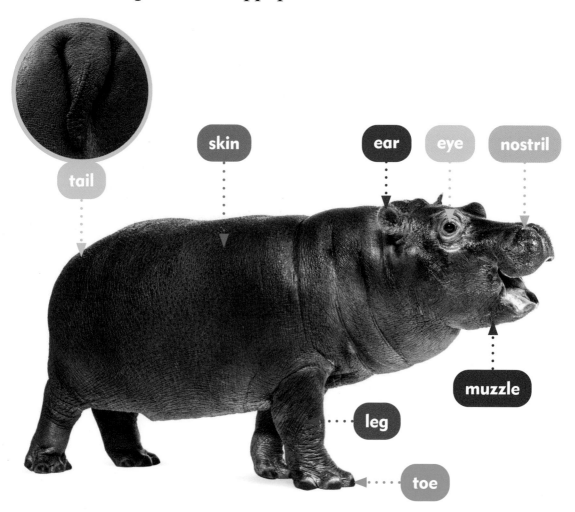

tail

skin

ear

eye

nostril

muzzle

leg

toe

Picture Glossary

bloat
A group of hippopotamuses.

calf
A young hippopotamus.

muzzle
An animal's nose and mouth.

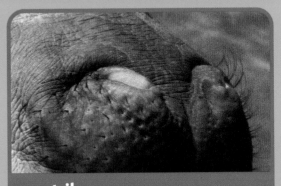

nostrils
The two openings of the nose that help a person or animal breathe and smell.

Index

To Learn More

FACT SURFER

Finding more information is as easy as 1, 2, 3.

❶ Go to www.factsurfer.com

❷ Enter "hippopotamuscalves" into the search box.

❸ Choose your book to see a list of websites.